LEGENDARY ADVENTURES

OF THE

BASEBALL FAN

CHRIS STANISCI, CPA

To order additional copies of this book, contact:
Xlibris
1-888-795-4274
www.Xlibris.com
Orders@Xlibris.com

ISBN: Softcover   978-1-7960-7341-6
        Hardcover   978-1-7960-7342-3
        EBook   978-1-7960-7340-9

Library of Congress Control Number: 2019919566

Print information available on the last page

Rev. date: 12/27/2019

DEDICATION PAGE

To My Baby Girl Christa and My Wife Michelle,

Little Christa I know you don't understand this book right now but someday you will.

You are such an amazing little girl with a heart like a lion just to survive. You are the most amazing little girl I've ever seen, and Daddy wants to make you a proud little girl.

Someday you will read this book and maybe a few more and know that this book is for you. Daddy loves you and your mother. I know your mother went through a lot while giving birth to you. I will always be grateful to her for that.

A special thanks to my friends Stevi Schnoor (Legend's Football League), Melissa Zemke (Financial Professional and a Model), and Giovanny Valencia (Hooters Around the World Facebook Fanpage).

FOREWORD

Prior to 2019 I visited a few ballparks in the country — most notably the home of the 2018 World Series champions, Fenway Park; Los Angeles Dodgers Stadium; the Ballpark at Arlington; Orioles Park at Camden Yards; and the home of the 2019 World Series champions, Nationals Park in Washington, DC. Therefore these ballparks are not included within this book as this book is devoted to the twenty-four ballparks visited during 2019.

The first stadium visited was Tropicana Field (home of the Tampa Bay Rays) on Opening Day 2019 (a matchup featuring 2018 Cy Young Winner Blake Snell versus the two-time and 2019 Cy Young Award Winner Justin Verlander) with a friend from college. Subsequent to this visit, a different friend from Texas asked that I meet him in Houston for game 5 of the NBA Playoffs between the Houston Rockets and the Golden State Warriors. While in Houston, I visited Minute Maid Park to see Houston Astros baseball.

After completing visits to both Minute Maid Park in Houston and Tropicana Field in Saint Petersburg, I decided to visit ballparks within driving distance of my home in Chipley, Florida, that included revisiting Marlins Park in Miami and SunTrust Field in Atlanta for the first time, although I had previously visited the Atlanta Braves' former home, Turner Field. After visiting the four ballparks previously mentioned in 2019 and the other ballparks visited in prior years, an interest had spurred in visiting ballparks around the country.

The adventure began by visiting the website www.ballparkchasers.com. After reviewing this website, I set out to visit four ballparks in the Midwest: Kauffman Stadium in Kansas City, Wrigley Field in Chicago, Busch Stadium in St. Louis, and Miller Park in Milwaukee. Later, after talking with several friends, I decided to include PNC Park in Pittsburgh, a follow-up visit to Progressive Field in Cleveland, and first-time visits to Comerica Field in Detroit, Target Field in Minneapolis, and Coors Field in Denver. The travel was budgeted based on cheapest flights in and out of Chicago from Fort Myers and from Chicago to Denver. To also save money on travel, the least expensive Airbnbs were used in each city. The initial trip included landing in Chicago at night and on the following day driving to Kansas City for a nighttime baseball game. Then there was a day game in Chicago and another night game in Milwaukee the very next day. Upon posting my itinerary on the Ballparks Chasers fan page about making a day game in Chicago following a night game in Kansas City, I was snickered at by a couple of fellow ballpark chasers for making an impossible overnight journey. However, sure enough, I was able to make it both Wrigley Field and Miller Park the following days.

Following those two ballgames were the most amazing two days of baseball I've ever witnessed. In St. Louis, I saw the return of Albert Pujols to St. Louis in a Los Angeles Angels of Anaheim jersey. Not only was impressed with standing ovation after each at bat Pujols was able to hit a homerun and received sounding applause and took a curtain call. I'd never witnessed a visiting player receive that much attention. What a thing of beauty. The following day was also amazing. I witnessed a historic milestone not accomplished in over eighty years. The home team the Pittsburgh Pirates came back from two 3-run deficits in the ninth inning or later. The other ballparks on the trip in Cleveland, Detroit, and Minneapolis were completed without interruption except for averaging three or four hours of sleep per night. However, there was certainly a close call at Chicago O'Hare for a flight to Denver. After driving through the night from Minneapolis back to Chicago, I parked the car at the rental car facility and got to the gate. I arrived at the Frontier ticket counter with what the ticket agent told me was a minute to spare.

In any event, I was able to board the plane and head out to Denver, Colorado. Upon boarding the plane and during flight, I struck up a conversation with a beautiful young lady from Colorado. She asked if I had ever been to Denver, and I indicated no. She asked if she could show me around and gave me her phone number. When I landed in Denver, I informed a couple friends, and they advised me against it in fear that I might be robbed. However, leave it to me, I decided to acknowledge the young lady and called her and told her I was interested. She took me for a fun adventure through tunnels in the mountains to Idaho Falls where I treated her to lunch. So grateful I decided against heading my friend's advice. What a beautiful young lady. The day concluded with a visit to Coors Field for what was to be the final game of the trip and a flight back to Panama City the next morning.

However, the next morning, I had woken up in Denver subsequent to the planes departure back to Panama City. I headed to Denver Airport to try to figure out what to do. Turns out, after looking at the schedule of all the West Coast teams' ballparks I hadn't visited, I noticed

I could fit them all in and complete the ballpark tour of the West Coast, so I booked a flight from Denver to San Francisco and another cheap red-eye flight from Seattle back to Tampa with visits to ballparks in San Francisco, Anaheim, San Diego, Oakland, and Seattle. Just got lucky that all those teams had home games during this stretch of time. Upon arriving back in Tampa, that was supposed to be the end of the journey.

Of course I was also scheduled to be in New York for my cousin Jonathan's wedding in August. It just so happened that the three teams in the Northeast that I had yet to visit their new stadiums—the New York Yankees, Philadelphia Phillies, and New York Mets—all had home games that weekend. Thank you, Jonathan. Now certainly, after getting back to Florida from this wedding, that was certain to be the end of ballpark chasing 2019. But no, I noticed the Cincinnati Reds and Chicago White Sox were both at home around the same time at the end of September, so I decided to go there. While in Chicago, I noticed that my home team, the Tampa Bay Rays, had a chance to clinch a playoff berth in Toronto. Hey, instead of driving from Chicago back home to Chipley, I decided to call the US Border security and inquire what was need to enter Canada. They indicated to get a copy of my birth certificate since I already had a US passport, albeit expired. So my wife texted me a copy of the birth certificate that I proceeded to print out and handed to Canadian customs. This allowed me entry into Canada and the opportunity to see the Tampa Bay Rays clinch their spot to the 2019 playoffs. The first playoff birth since 2013. In Toronto I ran into the principal owner of the Tampa Bay Rays and was with him when the Rays punched their ticket to the 2019 playoffs. An amazing end to ballpark chasing 2019 concluded with Rays playoff games in St. Petersburg and Houston.

In 2020 I will conclude visiting all thirty current MLB ballparks with visits to Chase Field in Arizona and the Texas Rangers' new ballpark in Arlington, Texas.

TAMPA BAY RAYS

Tampa Bay Rays vs Houston Astros, Opening Day 2019

2018 Cy Young Winner Blake Snell vs 2019 Cy Young Winner Justin Verlander

Tampa Bay Rays cheerleaders

Tampa Bay Rays
mascots, Raymond
and D.J. Kitty

Watching Ray baseball
with friends watching
Rays baseball

My friends with Raymond

MIAMI MARLINS

Miami Marlins mascot, Billy

Miami Marlins cheerleaders

Visiting my cousin and his dad to celebrate my cousin's daughter's one-year-old birthday prior to the Marlins game. Picked up a Billy the Marlin bubblehead for him.

HOUSTON ASTROS

Houston Astros cheerleaders

Houston Astros mascot, Orbit

Watching Houston Astros baseball with a friend

ATLANTA BRAVES

Atlanta Braves cheerleaders

KANSAS CITY ROYALS

Kansas City Royals cheerleaders

Kansas City Royals mascot, Slugerrr

The fountains at Kauffman Stadium

CHICAGO CUBS

Chicago Cubs Mascot Clark

Wrigley Field

The Bean In Chicago

Chicago Riverwalk

MILWAUKEE BREWERS

Milwaukee Brewers mascot, Bernie, inside Miller Park

ST. LOUIS CARDINALS

St. Louis Cardinals mascot, Fred Bird

The Gateway Arch

Inside PNC Park

Pittsburgh at Sunrise

Beautiful sunrise from the top of the Duquesne Incline

CLEVELAND INDIANS

Cleveland Indians Striker Girls

Progressive Field

Enjoying Cedar Point in Sandusky, Ohio

NFL Hall of Fame In Canton

DETROIT TIGERS

Detroit Tigers stadium analyst and Detroit Tigers mascot, Paws

Detroit Tigers cheerleaders

MINNESOTA TWINS

Mall of America

Target Field

COLORADO ROCKIES

Colorado Rockies mascot, Dinger

Coors Field at Sunset

SAN FRANCISCO GIANTS

Golden Gate Bridge and outside Oracle Park with bubblehead

Golden Gate Bridge all Lit Los Angeles Angels of Anheim

LOS ANGELES ANGELS OF ANAHEIM

Grumman Chinese Theater, Star on Hollywood Walk of Fame, Cosplay Girls in Hollywood, and LA Angels of Anaheim cheerleaders

SAN DIEGO PADRES

Seals lounging in La Jolla Cove

San Diego Padres cheerleaders

OAKLAND ATHLETICS

Oakland Athletics mascot, Stomper, and Oakland Athletics stadium analyst

Redwood Forest National Park—giant sequoia

SEATTLE MARINERS

Seattle public market and Seattle Space Needle

Seattle Mariners Moose

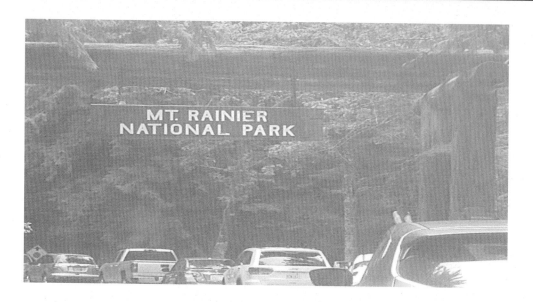

NEW YORK YANKEES

Empire State Building from Times Square, Statue of Liberty
from Staten Island Ferry, and Yankees Stadium

Freedom Tower from the Staten Island Ferry

Statue of Liberty

NEW YORK METS

New York Mets stadium analyst

New York Mets mascot, Mr. Met

Montauk Lighthouse

My cousin's wedding in New York, with his sister.

PHILADELPHIA PHILLIES

Philadelphia Eagles cheerleaders, Liberty Bell, and Citizens Bank Ballpark

Independence Hall

CINCINATTI REDS

Great American Ballpark, and Hooters' Miss February Sidney
on the day she found out she was in the Calendar

Mammoth Caves National Park

CHICAGO WHITE SOX

Chicago White Sox cheerleader

Guaranteed Rate Field

TORONTO BLUE JAYS

Entering into Canada through Windsor, Ontario

Overlooking Downtown Detroit from Windsor, Ontario

Stu Sternberg, owner of the Tampa Bay Rays, in Toronto
the day the rays clinched a playoff berth

And Toronto Blue Jays cheerleaders

Toronto Blue Jays mascot, Ace, inside the Rogers Center

CN Tower in Toronto

Hooters Toronto airport location

Visiting Niagara Falls on the way back into the United States

Visiting my uncle and his great-grandson in Cairo, New York, on the way back to Florida

Visiting my cousin's daughter in Saratoga Springs, New York, on the way back to Florida

Saratoga Spa State Park's signage at entryway

Saratoga Downs' oldest horse track in the United States with the newly built clubhouse

THE DRIVE SOUTH FROM UPSTATE NEW YORK TO FLORIDA

Baltimore's Inner Harbor

Lincoln Memorial in Washington, DC

Washington Monument in DC

Lincoln Memorial

Miss May 2020 – Angela of Naples

Siesta Key Beach, Sarasota, Florida

Hooters calendar girls of Sarasota

Miss July 2020 Alex

Miss November 2019 Feature Kelsey and Miss December 2019 Feature Alyssa

Covergirl and 2019 Miss Hooters International Brianna

Centerfold Gianna

My personal trainer at LA Fitness Elle

Back with my dad in Cape Coral, Florida

Watching Tampa Bay Rays' baseball playoff

Printed in the United States
By Bookmasters